T0020738

John Crossingham & Bobbie Kalman

Photographs by Marc Crabtree

Crabtree Publishing Company

www.crabtreebooks.com

Created by Bobbie Kalman

Dedicated by Kathy Kantor
Dla mojej kochanej Babci Zosi.

Editor-in-Chief
Bobbie Kalman

Writing team
John Crossingham
Bobbie Kalman

Substantive editor
Amanda Bishop

Project editor
Robin Johnson

Editors
Molly Aloian
Kelley MacAulay
Kathryn Smithyman

Design
Katherine Kantor
Samantha Crabtree (cover)

Production coordinator
Heather Fitzpatrick

Photo research
Crystal Foxton

Consultant
Sensei Kawasaki Kodokan Shichidan (7th Dan)
Kawasaki Rendokan Judo Academy, www.rendokan.ca

Special thanks to
Sensei Kawasaki for his many contributions to this book; McKenzie Arner, Anastasia Balach, Andrew Balach, Jay Campbell, Amanda Felker, Jean-Lucas Ferreira, Delaney Forsyth, Barbara Karpinski, Melanie Knezevic, Steve Knezevic, Raeanne McAlpine, Karlie Pereira, Nicklaus Tessaro, Vincent Tessaro, Madison Varga, and all their parents

Illustrations
Katherine Kantor: pages 6, 29, 30
Trevor Morgan: page 8
Bonna Rouse: pages 9, 10, 11, 14

Photographs and reproductions
All photographs by Marc Crabtree except:
Design by Marco Gagnon, © martialgraphics.com: page 4 (bottom)

Crabtree Publishing Company
www.crabtreebooks.com 1-800-387-7650

Cataloging-in-Publication Data
Crossingham, John.
Judo in action / John Crossingham & Bobbie Kalman; photographs by Marc Crabtree.
p. cm. -- (Sports in action series)
Includes index.
ISBN-13: 978-0-7787-0342-6 (rlb)
ISBN-10: 0-7787-0342-8 (rlb)
ISBN-13: 978-0-7787-0362-4 (pbk)
ISBN-10: 0-7787-0362-2 (pbk)
1. Judo--Juvenile literature. I. Kalman, Bobbie. II. Crabtree, Marc. III. Title. IV. Sports in action.
GV1114.C76 2006
796.815'2--dc22
2005019991
LC

Published in the United States
PMB16A
350 Fifth Ave.
Suite 3308
New York, NY
10118

Published in Canada
616 Welland Ave.,
St. Catharines, Ontario,
Canada
L2M 5V6

Published in the United Kingdom
73 Lime Walk
Headington
Oxford
OX3 7AD
United Kingdom

Published in Australia
386 Mt. Alexander Rd.,
Ascot Vale (Melbourne)
VIC 3032

Contents

What is judo? 柔道

Judo is a physical sport, but it is also a peaceful art. In Japanese, the word "judo" means "gentle way."

Judo is a **martial art**, or a fighting style that can be used for self-defense. It is also an Olympic sport. Students of judo are called ***judoka***. Through training and **discipline**, judoka learn how to defend themselves against attacks. They learn how to turn the movements and strength of their **opponents** back against the opponents. Judoka also learn about respect. True judoka never use their skills to attack—only for self-defense.

A martial art for everyone

Judo began in Japan in 1882. It was created by Master Jigoro Kano, shown left. Kano was a student of **jujitsu**, an aggressive martial art used by **samurai warriors**. Kano soon began designing his own martial art. His goal was to create a martial art that could be used by all people, regardless of their size or strength. He replaced jujitsu's aggressive kicks and punches with safer throwing and falling **techniques** *(waza)*. Kano started a judo school called **Kodokan**, and judo was born.

*Judo became popular when Master Kano and his students were challenged by a police chief in Tokyo to compete against jujitsu students. Kano's students won the **competition**. Many people soon joined his Kodokan school.*

The principles of judo

Judoka learn the two principles of judo: ***jita-kyoe*** and ***seiryoku-zenyo***. Jita-kyoe means valuing the health and well-being of all people, including opponents. Seiryoku-zenyo means using energy efficiently while practicing judo.

Known around the world

There is only one style of judo in the world—Kodokan judo. It is based on Kano's original teachings. Judo became an official men's Olympic sport in 1964 and an official women's Olympic sport in 1992. Today, judo is practiced by people around the world for sport, exercise, and self-defense.

Glossary of Japanese words

In this book, you will find many Japanese words commonly used in judo. This glossary will help you keep track of the meanings of some of the words that appear often throughout the book.

dojo A training hall where judo classes are held

judogi A judo uniform

judoka A judo student or students

randori Judo practice sessions

sensei A judo teacher

tatami Mats on the floor of a dojo

tori A person performing a judo technique

uke A person receiving a judo technique

Judoka train hard many times a week.

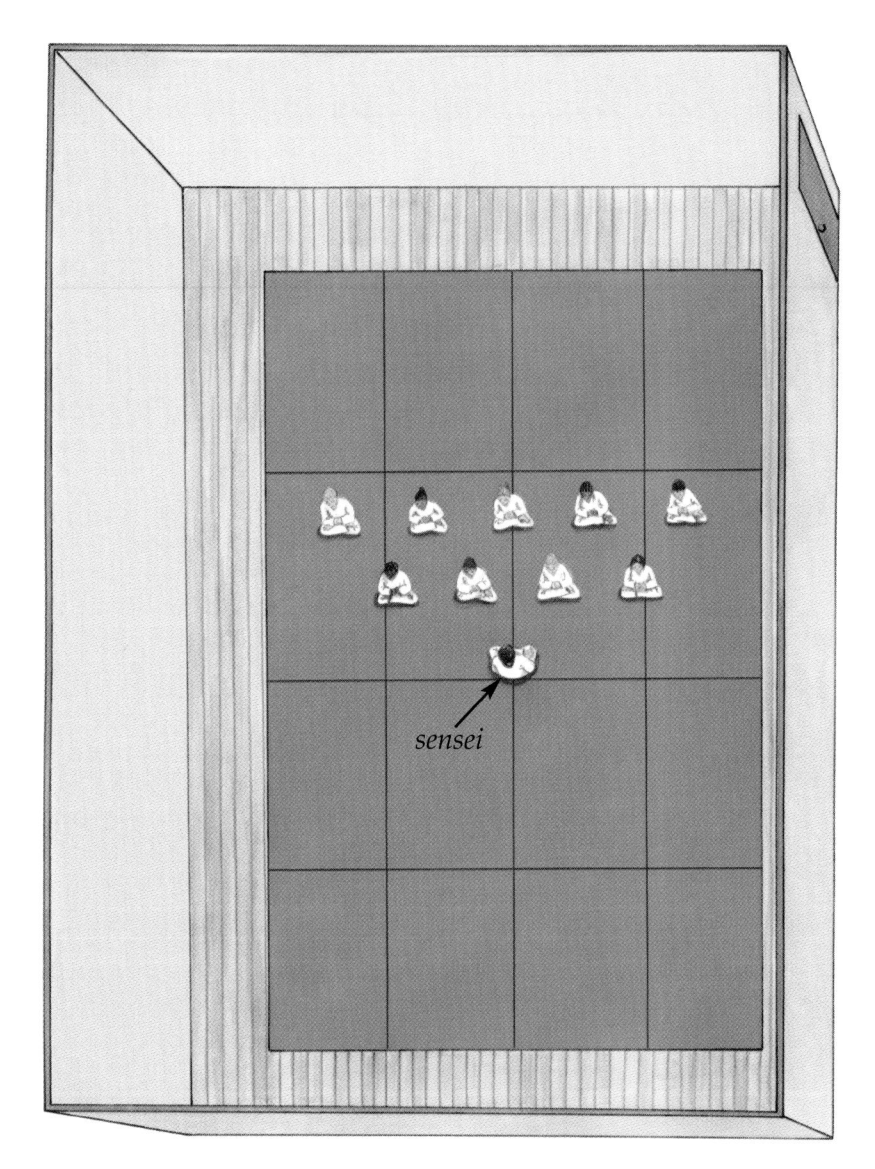

In the dojo

Judo **sessions**, or classes, take place in a large training hall called a *dojo*. In Japanese, the word "dojo" means "school." In the dojo, judoka learn and practice judo moves and techniques. Practice sessions are called *randori*. Randori is supervised by a *sensei*. The sensei is the judo teacher who is in charge of the dojo. Judoka give the sensei their attention and respect.

A dojo usually has a wooden floor. The floor is covered by tatami, *or mats. The mats help cushion judoka's falls.*

Mind your manners

Judo has a code of **etiquette**, or acceptable behavior. All judoka must behave properly when they are in the dojo. Some points of judo etiquette are listed below.

- Always show respect for your sensei and for higher-ranking judoka.
- Shoes are not allowed in the dojo.
- Remove jewelry or any other sharp objects that could injure you or others.
- Talking is not allowed during a judo session, unless the sensei is speaking to you.
- Be mindful of your fellow judoka. Injuring a fellow judoka by being careless or mean is not the judo way!

Showing respect

Always bow to the sensei and to the **Kano Shihan** before entering or leaving the dojo. Kano Shihan is Jigoro Kano's title as the founder of judo. In most dojo, his picture hangs on a wall. By bowing, you show respect for him, for your sensei, and for the **customs** of judo. There are two types of bows—kneeling bows and standing bows.

1. To perform a kneeling bow (zarei), *begin in a kneeling position with your toes touching. Place your hands on your upper thighs, with your fingers pointing inward.*

2. Bend forward at the waist. Place your palms flat on the floor in front of your knees with your fingers pointing inward.

To perform a standing bow (ritsurei), *stand with your heels together and bend forward at the waist. Keep your arms straight and rest your fingertips on your upper thighs. Judoka perform this bow when they face their opponents.*

What you need 柔道

The long-sleeved top of a judogi looks like a jacket. It is fastened by a belt.

The most important equipment a judoka needs is a uniform called a *judogi*. The pants and top of a judogi are loose-fitting and made of cotton. Judogi are usually white, but some are blue. The judogi may look lightweight, but it is **durable**, or long-lasting. It is designed to withstand training and competitions. A judoka must always keep his or her judogi clean and neat.

Stay cool

Remember to take small drinks of water often throughout your judo session. Drinking water helps keep your body **hydrated** and full of energy.

Belts of many colors

white belt

black belt

The colored belts worn in judo show each student's **grade**, or skill level. Judoka begin with white belts and then progress to yellow, orange, green, blue, brown or purple, and black belts. Judoka must be at least ten years old to be tested for their green belts and at least twelve years old to be tested for their brown or purple belts.

Black belts

Black belts are called ***dans***. They are the highest belts that judoka can achieve. There are ten levels of black belts. Judoka cannot try for their first-level black belts until they are at least fifteen years old.

yellow belt

orange belt

green belt

blue belt

brown or purple belt

Striped belts

The belts worn in judo are usually a solid color. Some female judoka, however, wear belts with white stripes on them. Wearing striped belts is a tradition that began in the Kodokan school. Female competitors wore belts with stripes to set themselves apart from male competitors. Today, more and more female judoka wear belts that are a solid color.

Warming up 柔道

Your body must be **flexible** to perform judo moves well. The sensei begins each session with stretches that will help prevent injuries by increasing your flexibility. Stretches warm up your muscles and get your heart pumping. Try the stretches on this page to warm up your body. Only stretch as far as you can without feeling pain, however. In time, you'll find that you can stretch farther than you could in the past. Once you have stretched your muscles, you can begin strengthening them. Try some of the strengthening exercises shown on the next page. They will help you become more powerful.

Calf stretch

Begin the calf stretch with your feet shoulder-width apart. Take a big step forward with one foot, keeping the other foot flat on the floor. Bend the knee of your front leg until it is directly above your ankle. Place your hands on the thigh of your front leg for support. Keep the heel of your back foot on the floor. Lean your upper body forward. You should feel the stretch in the calf muscle of your back leg. Hold this position and count to ten. Now stretch the other leg.

"V" stretch

To perform this stretch, sit with your legs in a "V" position. Flex your feet so your toes are pointing upward. While keeping your lower back straight, lean forward. You will feel the stretch in the back of your legs and buttocks. Hold this position as you count to ten.

Pushups

To perform a pushup, first lie on your stomach. Place your hands flat on the floor under your shoulders. Use your arms to push up your body, keeping your back flat. Then lower your body until your nose is about four inches (10 cm) from the floor. Do this ten times. Rest. Try to do several **sets** of pushups, resting after each set. If you find the exercise too difficult with your legs straight, keep your knees on the floor as you push up.

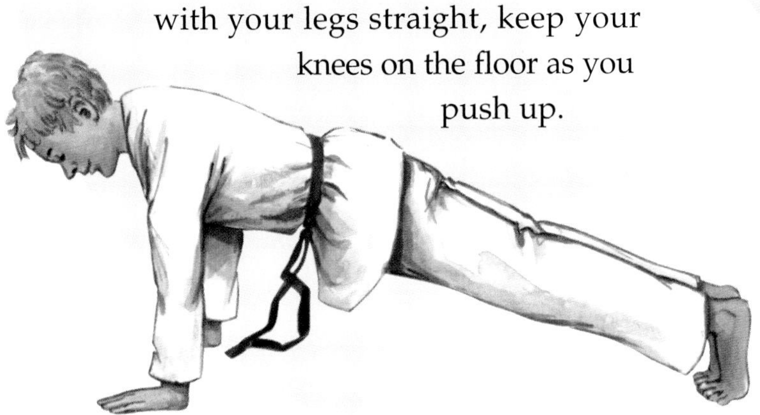

Crunches

Begin by lying on your back with your hands behind your head. Bend your knees and place your feet flat on the floor. Keeping your lower back pressed against the floor, slowly lift your upper body slightly off the floor. Then lower yourself back to the floor. Repeat this exercise ten times. Rest. Try to do several sets of crunches, resting after each set.

Calm down

Judo is as much about the mind as it is about the body. To "stretch" your mind, your sensei will often ask you to take part in **meditation** (*mokuso*) at the beginning and end of each class. At the start of class, meditation helps clear your thoughts so you can focus on judo. At the end of class, meditation allows you to think about everything you have learned that day. It also gives your body a chance to cool down.

To meditate, sit in the meditation position shown above. Close your eyes and focus on taking deep, full breaths.

Judo basics 柔道

There are a lot of judo moves, but each move belongs to one of four categories—**throws**, **holds**, **locks**, and **chokes**. Each move offers a different way to gain control over your opponent. A throw takes your opponent down to the floor. A hold keeps your opponent on the ground. A lock increases the pressure on your opponent so he or she will give up. A choke applies pressure to your opponent's neck. Chokes are advanced moves that can be performed only by **senior judoka**, so they are not shown in this book.

The right stance

Judo is all about keeping your own balance as you force your opponent to lose his or her balance. Good balance begins with the right **stance**. A stance is the position of your entire body, including your legs, feet, arms, hands, and head. There are two stances to learn—natural stance (*hon-shizentai*), and defensive stance (*jigotai*).

Natural stance

Natural stance allows you to move quickly into action. To stand in natural stance, turn one foot to the side and place it slightly behind you. Place your other foot slightly ahead of you, so your toes point forward. Lift up your arms and bend your elbows. Your hands should be about chest-height, with your fingers curled slightly toward you. Keep your body upright.

Defensive stance

Defensive stance provides great balance and protection. To stand in defensive stance, begin in natural stance. Spread your feet farther apart. Bend your knees and lean forward at the hips. Hold your hands up in front of your body. Keep your head up.

A gripping tale

In judo, it is important to know how to get a good **grip** (*kumikata*). A grip is the handhold that you use when you grab your opponent's judogi. Once you have a firm grip, you can move your body into position to perform a throw. At first, you will practice various grips. Later, you can use the grips during randori.

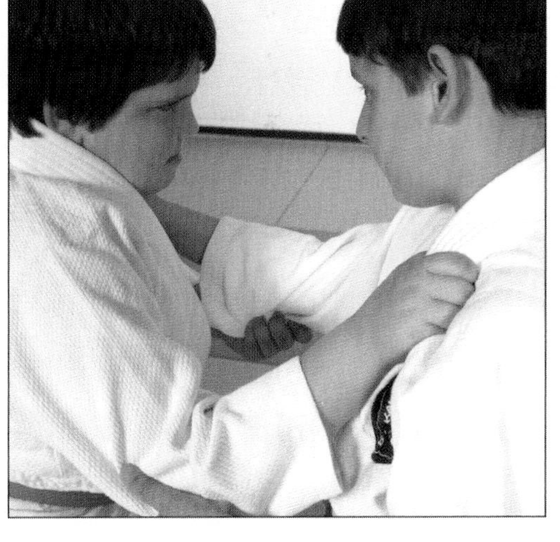

A basic grip

To perform a basic grip, begin in natural stance. Grip your opponent's collar (*eri*) with one hand. Now, take your other hand and grip his or her sleeve (*sode*) near the elbow. Keep your feet steady. Stay relaxed by breathing normally. Remember that both you and your opponent are trying to get a good grip on each other.

A judogi is designed to be gripped in several places. The collar, sleeves, and underarms of your top are especially sturdy.

Breakfalls 柔道

Every judoka must fall. A basic part of your training is learning how to fall without getting hurt. Safe falls are called **breakfalls** (*ukemi*). Breakfalls are intentional falls that prevent your head from hitting the ground. By using a breakfall, you will be in control of your body when you hit the mat. Being in control allows you to move quickly into position to fight off your opponent. There are four main styles of breakfalls—front breakfalls, side breakfalls, rear breakfalls, and forward rolling breakfalls. You can practice these moves alone at first, but make sure you are on the tatami!

Front breakfall

Although a front breakfall (*mae-ukemi*) seems simple, it is quite difficult. You must avoid falling on your knees during this breakfall.

Fall forward, extending your arms in front of you with the palms of your hands facing down. Your palms and forearms will hit the mat first. Do not land on your knees. Keep your head and hips off the mat.

Side breakfall

You will often get thrown down on your side in judo. Be sure to practice side breakfalls (*yoko-ukemi*) on both your right and left sides.

1. To perform a side breakfall to the left side, squat down and throw your left arm up and out. Push your left leg across your body and roll to the left.

2. As your body hits the ground, slap the mat with your left arm. Tuck your chin into your chest to keep your head off the mat.

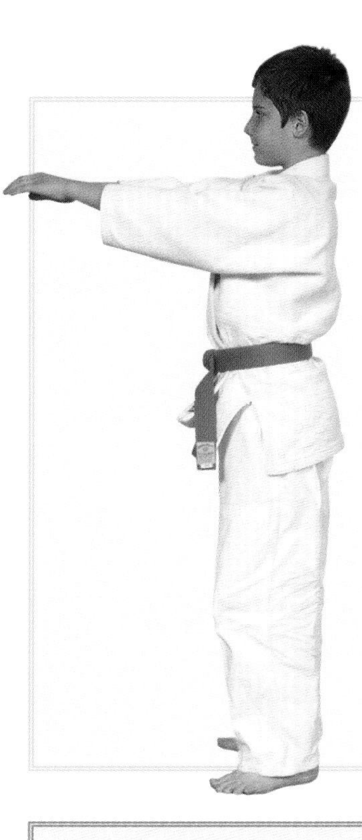

Rear breakfall

Performing the rear breakfall (*ushiro-ukemi*) will allow you to protect your back while falling.

1. Stand with your arms raised in front of your body. Bend your knees deeply as you allow yourself to fall backward. Keep your chin close to your chest as you fall.

2. When your lower back begins to hit the mat, slap both hands down onto the mat. This motion will keep your head and neck from hitting the ground.

Forward rolling breakfall

A forward rolling breakfall (*zempo-kaiten-ukemi*) is similar to a somersault. You can practice this breakfall by rolling over a partner.

1. To perform a forward rolling breakfall, begin by bending your knees and leaning forward. Keep your palms open.

2. As you fall forward, roll over onto one shoulder. Be sure to keep your chin tucked in as you roll.

3. At the end of the roll, slap your arm down onto the mat to stop yourself from rolling.

Throw down! 柔道

There are about 50 throws in judo. Each throw is designed to bring an opponent quickly to the ground. The three main types of throws are hand throws (*te-waza*), hip throws (*koshi-waza*), and leg throws (*ashi-waza*). The person performing the throw is called the *tori*. The person being thrown is known as the *uke*.

Unbalancing and balancing

To perform a throw well, you must do two things. First, you must unbalance your opponent. This technique is called ***kuzushi***. Second, your body must be in the proper position to stay balanced during the throw. This technique is called ***tsukuri***. While learning different throws, concentrate on doing these two things again and again. As you become more skilled at keeping your balance while unbalancing your opponent, your throws will improve.

Using the force

A great throw is about skill, not strength. As your opponent lunges forward to attack you, use the force of your opponent's movement to bring him or her down. The tori, shown below, is using his opponent's force to unbalance and throw the uke. With practice, you will learn to throw opponents safely—even those who are bigger and stronger than you are!

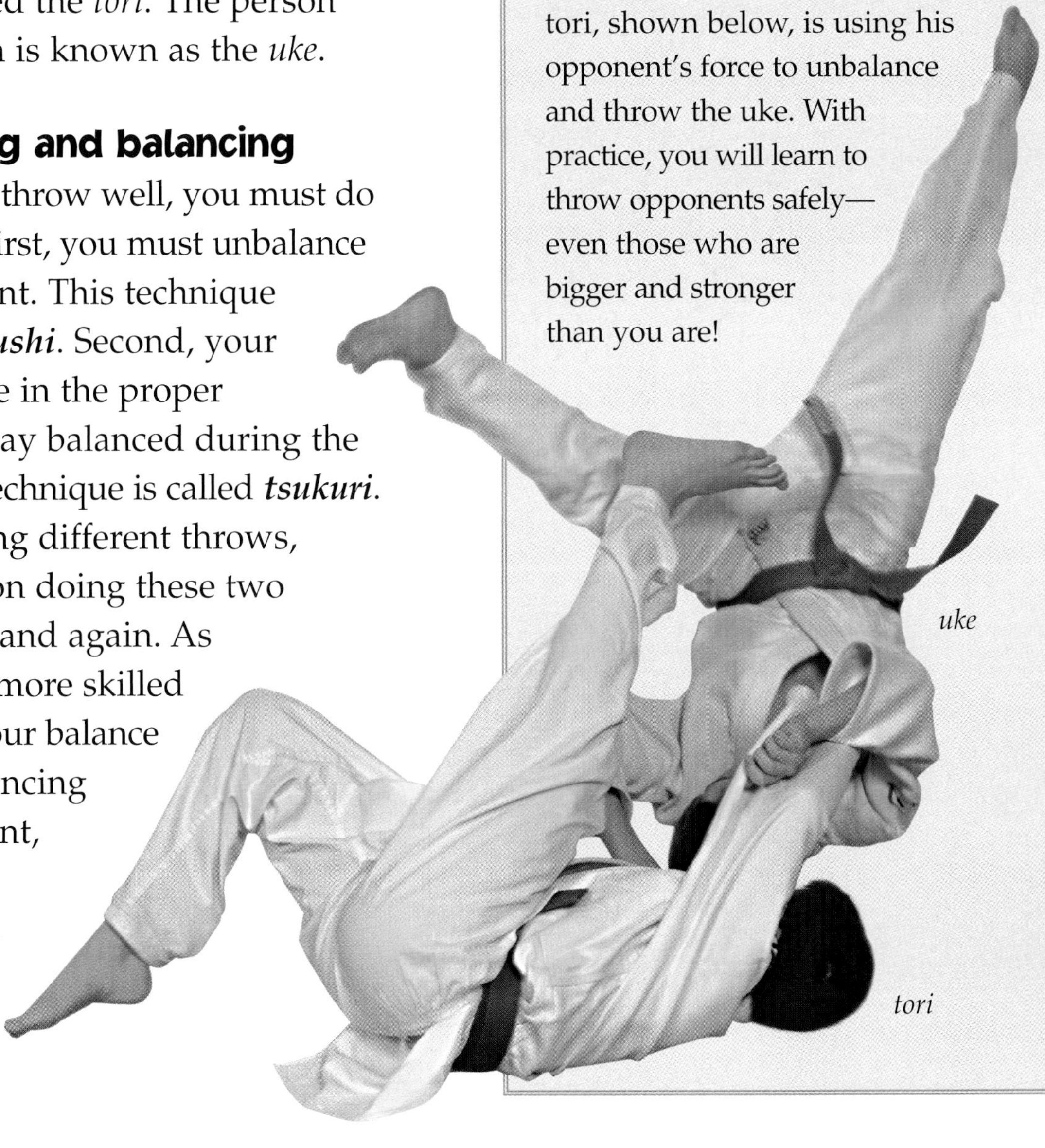

uke

tori

Body drop

The body drop (*tai-otoshi*) is one of the first hand throws you will learn.

1. To perform a body drop, grip your opponent by the collar and sleeve and push him or her backward. The uke will push forward to resist you. Now, quickly pull the uke toward you. Turn to your left and stick out your right leg.

2. Flip your opponent over your right leg and onto the ground. You can also turn to the right and flip the uke over your left leg.

Major hip throw

The major hip throw (*o-goshi*) is a throw commonly used by beginners. This move will show you the importance of a strong grip. Begin the major hip throw by facing your opponent.

1. Grab the uke's right sleeve as you quickly cross your right foot in front of your body. This motion will spin you around so that your back is to the uke.

2. Bend your knees. At the same time, sweep your right hand around the uke's back and grab his or her judogi at the hip. Now, straighten your legs, lean forward, and toss the uke over your hips and to the ground.

Sweeps and reaps

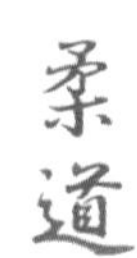

In leg throws, you use your legs to trip your opponent. There are two types of leg throws—**sweeps** and **reaps**. Sweeps are forward leg movements, and reaps are backward leg movements. Both types of leg throws can unbalance your opponent. You must then use a strong grip to bring him or her to the floor. The greatest challenge in a leg throw is to avoid kicking your opponent. Kicks are **fouls** in judo. Fouls are moves that are not allowed. Wrapping your leg around your opponent's leg is also a foul. Your sweep or reap must be a smooth, fluid motion.

Advancing foot sweep

The advancing foot sweep (*de-ashi-barai*) is a common leg throw in judo. It uses a motion similar to the push and pull motion used to perform the body drop on page 17.

1. To perform an advancing foot sweep, grip the uke (wearing the orange belt) by the collar and sleeve. Push the uke away from you and then take a step backward.

2. Just as the uke steps in to follow you, strongly sweep away the uke's left foot with your right foot.

3. Use your grip to unbalance the uke further and to drag him or her to the ground.

Major inner reap

Keep a tight grip on your opponent's collar as you perform the major inner reap (*o-uchi-gari*).

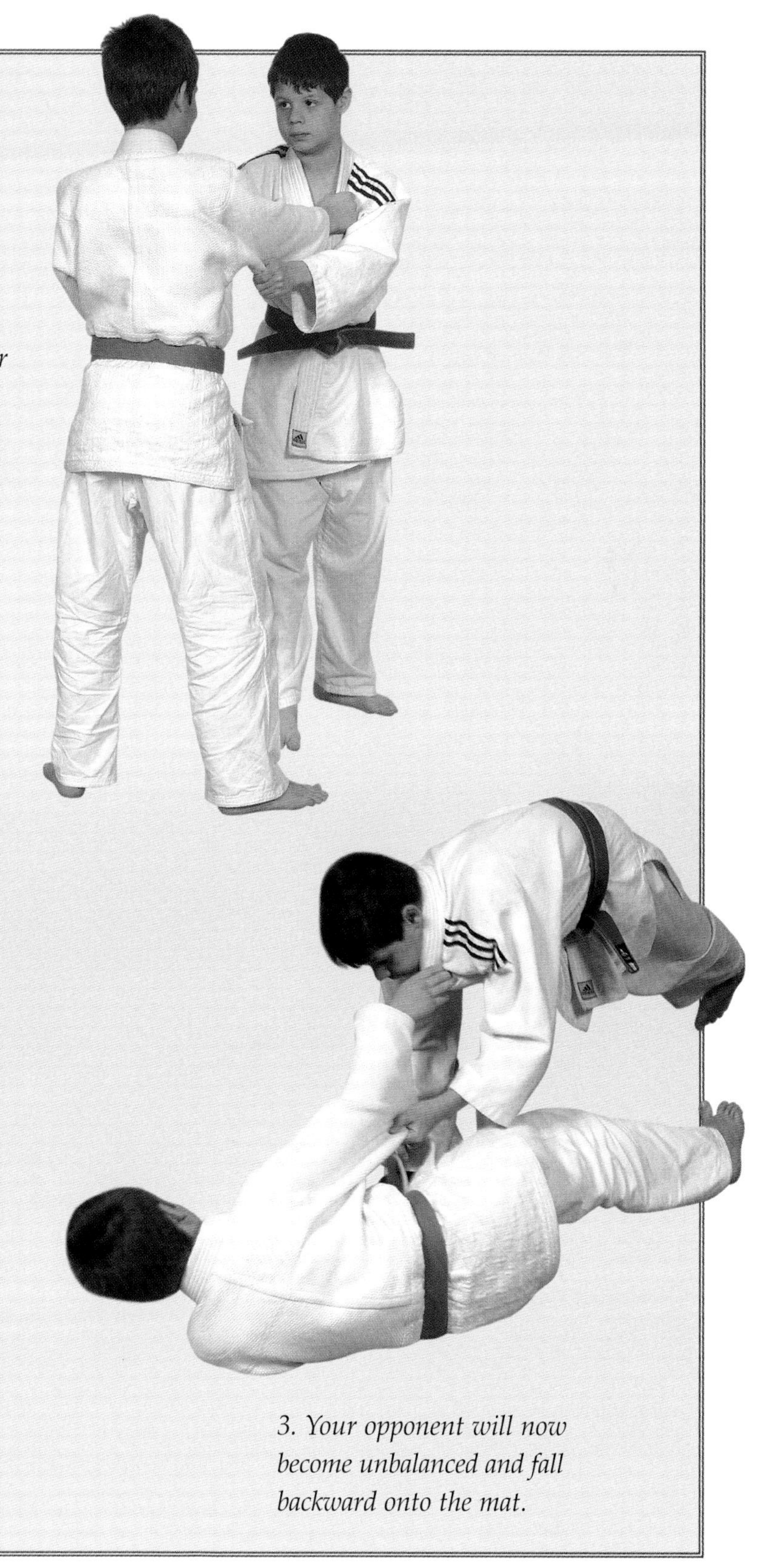

1. To perform a major inner reap using your right leg, grip the uke (wearing the solid white judogi) by his or her collar and sleeve.

2. Swing him or her around to the right. Quickly slip your right leg between the uke's legs and reap back his or her left leg. At the same time, pull down on the uke's collar.

3. Your opponent will now become unbalanced and fall backward onto the mat.

Laying the groundwork

Once you have thrown your opponent successfully to the mat, it is time for **groundwork**. Groundwork is made up of the **grappling**, or gripping, moves you perform on the tatami. Your goal is to stay in control of your opponent and stop him or her from getting back up. The best way to stay in control is by using holds (*ne-waza*).

While performing holds, position yourself so that you can use your body weight to help trap your opponent beneath you. Even strong judoka find it difficult to break well-placed holds. In competition, you can score a **hold-down** by keeping your opponent pinned to the mat for 25 seconds. A hold-down wins the **match**.

Scarf hold

The scarf hold (*kesa-gatame*) is one of the first holds judoka learn. It is a great move to make after you throw an opponent onto his or her back.

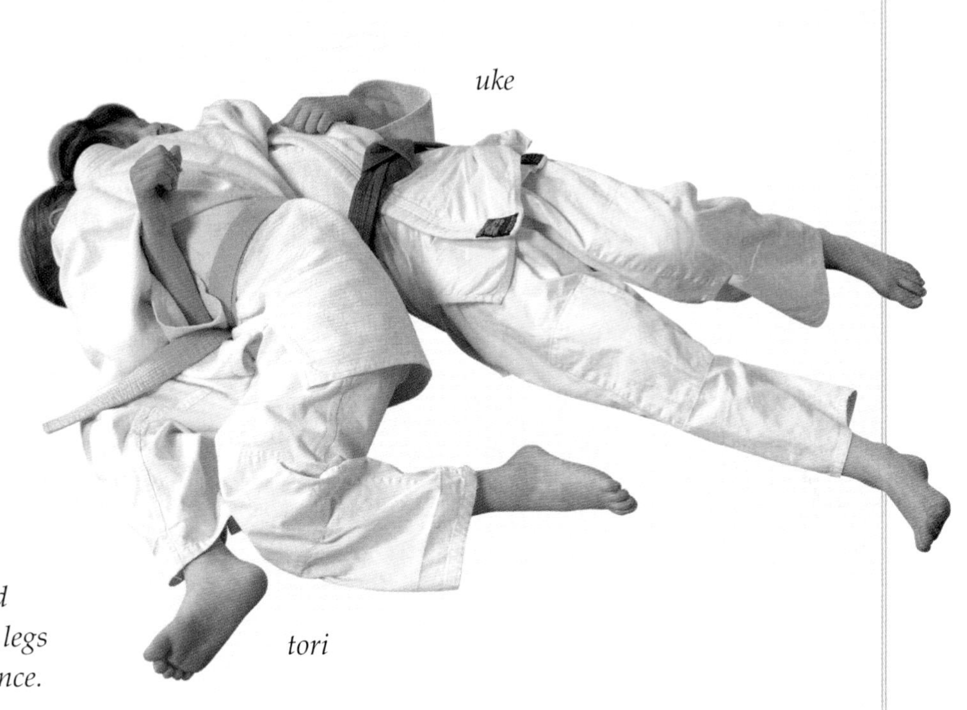

Lie across the uke's shoulder or chest. Place one hand under his or her neck. With your other hand, grab the uke's elbow. Squeeze that arm under your armpit as you bend over and trap your opponent. Spread your legs wide apart to maintain your balance.

Trunk hold

When you perform the trunk hold (*tate-shiho-gatame*), you use your full body weight to pin your opponent to the mat.

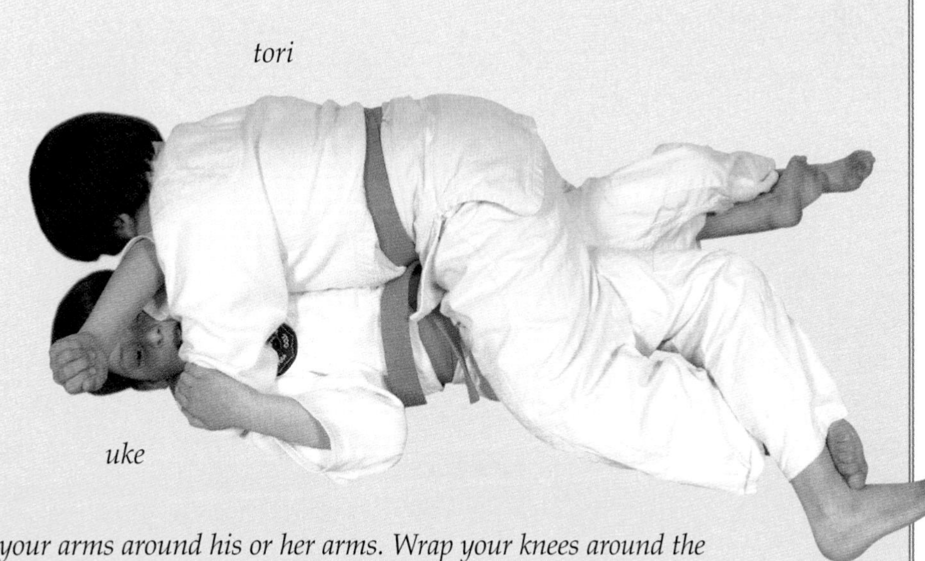

Sit on the uke's chest and wrap your arms around his or her arms. Wrap your knees around the uke's waist, with your toes pointing backward. If your opponent struggles free, pin the uke's arms back above his or her head. Lean forward and apply pressure to maintain the hold and prevent the uke from rolling onto his or her stomach.

All locked up 柔道

As judoka become more skilled, they are often able to escape from holds. As a result, their opponents must use stronger holds to control them. Strong holds are called locks (*kansetsu-waza*). Locks are also known as **vital point techniques** because they are used on key parts of the body. Most locks are performed on an opponent's arms, legs, or neck. Applying locks to these body parts gives a judoka control over his or her opponent. Even a skilled judoka cannot escape from a well-placed lock. A lock should never hurt your opponent, however. Locks can be very dangerous, and they must be used carefully to avoid injuries. For this reason, only senior judoka are allowed to perform locks.

The judoka in blue is applying a cross armlock (ude-hishigi-juji-gatame) *to her opponent.*

I give up!

Submission, or the act of giving up, is an essential part of judo. During a judo match, you submit to your opponent by giving a **submission signal**. To give a submission signal, tap your opponent or the mat twice with an open-palmed hand. When you do so, your opponent must release the move immediately. Obeying the submission signal helps keep judo safe for everyone.

*The uke in the white judogi cannot escape from his opponent's lock and is using the submission signal to give up. Many other rules exist to protect judoka from injuries. Ask your sensei about which moves are **illegal**, or not allowed, so you can practice safe judo.*

Solving problems 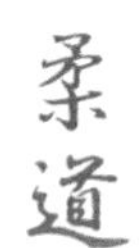

While facing an opponent, you must think fast. Otherwise, you will find yourself pinned down on the mat.

During randori, judoka are usually paired up with people of similar strength, body size, and skill level.

During each judo session, time is set aside for randori. Randori is a practice period during which students pair up to improve their skills. Each judoka practices throws, holds, and locks, combining techniques in an attempt to gain control over his or her opponent.

Think fast

Your opponent will not make it easy for you to attack him or her. For example, your first attempt at a throw may not be successful. When this happens, you must quickly change your attack to surprise your opponent. The more moves you know, the easier it is to gain control over your opponent. During randori, try as many new moves as possible. You will learn quickly which moves are your strongest and which skills you need to improve.

Smooth moves

A **combination** (*renraku-waza*) is a series of moves that is most effective when performed together. Moving smoothly and gracefully is the most important part of any combination. Do not get frustrated when you are learning how to link moves together. Only practice and study can improve your ability to make decisions while facing an opponent. If you are patient and hard-working, you'll soon find yourself performing quick combinations naturally. The moves shown on this page make up a common beginner combination.

1. The tori in blue is attempting a large outer reap (o-soto-gari). *She is trying to reap the uke's leg out from under him. Her opponent, however, is maintaining his balance. The uke is centered and standing strong.*

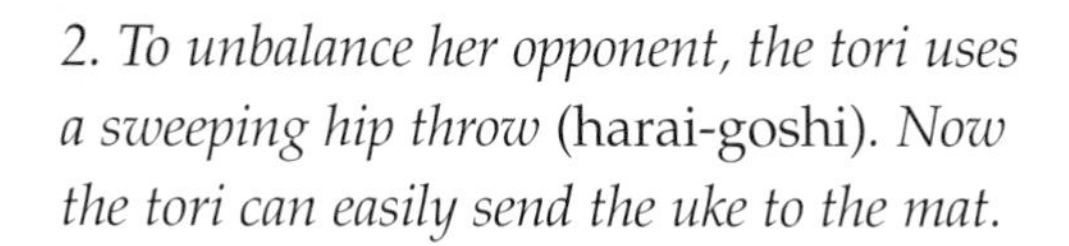

2. To unbalance her opponent, the tori uses a sweeping hip throw (harai-goshi). *Now the tori can easily send the uke to the mat.*

Turning the tables 柔道

Judo is all about using the strength of your opponent against him or her. **Countermoves** (*kaeshi-waza*) do just that. A countermove stops your opponent's attack and puts you into position to attack. If you think fast, you can gain control by reacting to a weak attack with a countermove.

For example, while attacking with a foot sweep, your opponent may be slightly off-balance. His or her foot is moving quickly in one direction. If you can hook that foot and sweep it farther in the same direction, you'll spin your opponent around. Then you will have gained control and can begin to attack.

1. The judoka in white is attempting a foot sweep on his opponent's right foot. The judoka in blue is making a countermove. She spins quickly to her right and keeps a strong grip on her opponent's judogi.

2. The judoka in blue throws her hip back into her opponent and performs a quick hip throw. Her opponent will soon be flat on the mat. In judo, the uke can become the tori in an instant.

Fooled you!

A **sacrifice throw** is not a countermove, but it has a similar effect. This move leads your opponent to believe that you are off-balance. Instead, you are leading your opponent into a throw. A sacrifice throw is risky. If you perform it too slowly or against a skilled opponent, you will soon be on your back and in danger of being pinned. Practice this move during randori, so that you can perform it with confidence.

The stomach throw can be an effective sacrifice throw. Lie on your back and hold on to your opponent's collar. Place your feet on his or her stomach and flip your opponent over your body.

Sensei knows best

If you are frustrated learning countermoves and sacrifice throws, ask your sensei for advice. The sensei will correct your techniques and suggest ways to improve your performance. The sensei, shown left, is instructing his students during randori.

Kata—body and mind 柔道

Master Kano believed that judo should focus on more than just fighting. He designed **kata**, or forms, to create a perfect balance between the body and the mind. Kata demonstrate the artistic side of judo. Each kata is a series of body motions performed in a specific pattern. Some kata include throws or holds, and some simulate self-defense moves. Others are designed to represent planets or forces of nature.

Focus and repetition

Kata are important for two reasons. First, these exercises help focus your mind. Second, as you repeat each motion, your body movements become stronger and smoother. Performing kata trains your mind and body to make quick, exact movements. A judoka who performs kata well is strong in competitions.

Many kata are performed in pairs.

Slow down!

Kata are performed slowly and with control. If judoka try to perform the motions too quickly, the kata become sloppy. First, it is important to learn the motions well. Over time, you can increase the speed and strength of the kata. These motions may seem simple, but they take years to perfect.

Seven kata

There are seven kata for you to learn. Most are designed to improve judoka's muscle strength, balance, and flexibility. Some kata, such as ***Ju-No-Kata***, or "forms of gentleness," can be performed alone. Other kata, such as ***Nage-No-Kata***, or "forms of throwing," are performed with a partner. In addition to performing gracefully, the students challenge each other by changing their attacking and defending forms during the kata.

Nage-No-Kata

Most kata are divided into sets of moves. In Nage-No-Kata, there are five sets of moves. Each set consists of three throws. The throws are performed to both the left and right sides. These illustrations show the first set of moves in Nage-No-Kata. They are called hand techniques (*te-waza*).

Floating Drop *(Uki-Otoshi)*

Shoulder Throw *(Seoi-Nage)*

Shoulder Wheel *(Kata-Guruma)*

Judo competitions 柔道

When you are ready, your sensei may invite you to enter a judo competition. Some competitions focus on kata, but most center around fighting. Judoka face off on a large square mat that is 8.75 yards (8 m) wide. A warning zone is part of the competition area. If a competitor crosses over the outside edge of the warning zone, he or she is **out of bounds**. The mat continues beyond the warning zone to provide a safety area for the competitors. There are two **judges** who keep score during each match, and a **referee** who ensures that the competitors follow the rules. Depending on the age group, certain moves may not be allowed. During a match, you may be asked to wear a belt that is a different color than your opponent's belt color—or even a full blue judogi. Doing so helps the judges tell you and your opponent apart.

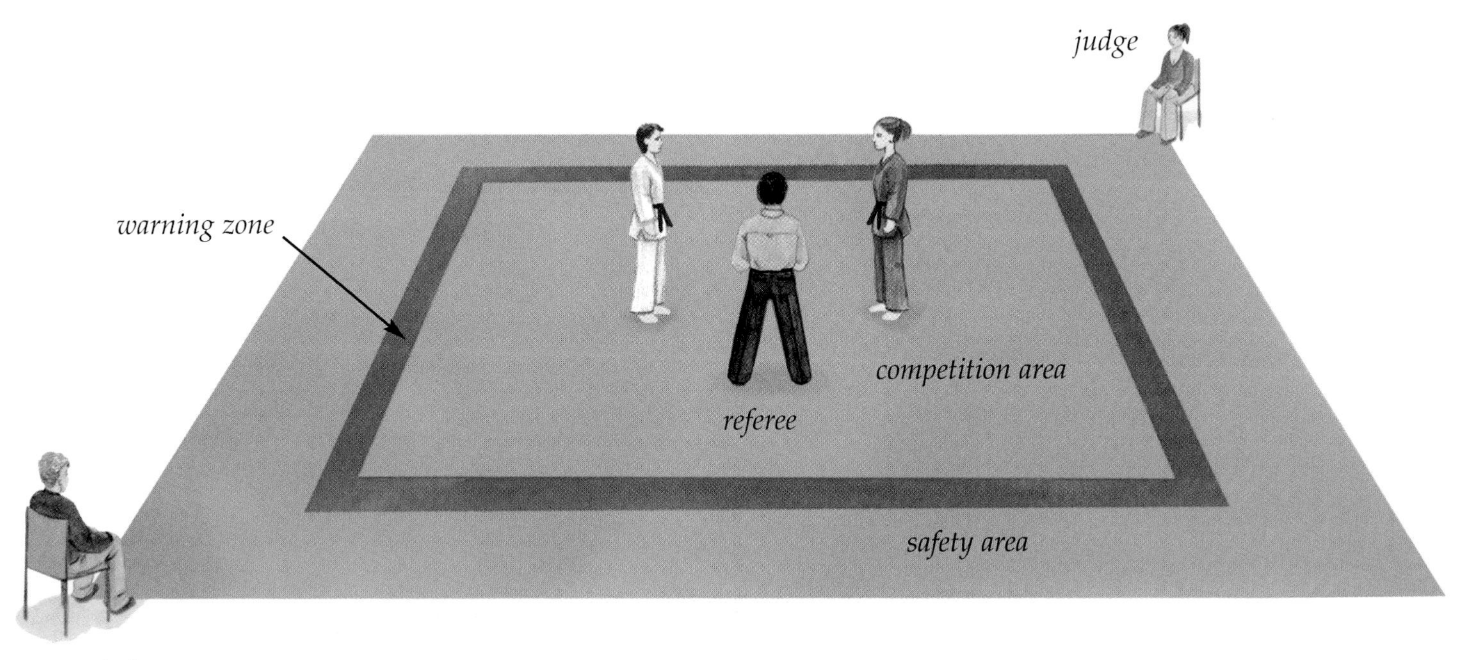

Junior judo matches are three minutes long. Senior judo matches last five minutes. Timekeepers are responsible for timing both the length of the match and the length of each hold used during the match.

What's the score?

Judges use a point system to determine the winner of a match. The simplest way to win a match is by scoring an ***ippon***. You can score an ippon by pinning your opponent down with a hold for 25 seconds, by getting your opponent to submit to a hold, or by using a powerful throw to land your opponent down on his or her back. The other point categories are listed below.

waza-ari—A hold lasting 20 to 24 seconds or a throw that puts an opponent down almost entirely on his or her back

yuko—A hold lasting 15 to 19 seconds or a throw that puts an opponent down on his or her side

koka—A hold lasting 10 to 14 seconds or a throw that puts an opponent down on his or her bottom or thigh

penalty points—Points can be deducted if the referee or judges see an illegal move such as a kick.

Add it up!

A competitor wins the match immediately, if he or she scores an ippon. If no one scores an ippon by the end of the match, the judges add up the other points scored by each competitor. A waza-ari is worth more than a yuko, and a yuko is worth more than a koka. Even if a competitor scored several koka, his or her opponent would win the match with just one higher-level yuko. In judo matches, the higher-level categories always beat the lower-level categories.

Competitions test your ability to use combinations and countermoves to surprise your opponent.

A referee uses hand signals to control the match and to award points to competitors.

Glossary

Note: Boldfaced words that are defined in the text may not appear in the glossary.

competition An organized contest in which people compete or try to win by defeating the other participants

custom A traditional way of behaving that has become accepted by people

discipline Training that develops skill and proper behavior

flexible Able to bend one's body easily

hydrated Having the right amount of water in one's body

match Two judoka facing off against each other to fight

meditation An exercise that calms you and focuses your mind

opponent The person against whom a judoka is fighting in a judo practice session or match

out of bounds The area outside the competition area in a judo match

samurai warriors Fighters who belonged to a powerful military class in Japan during medieval times

senior judoka Judo students who are sixteen years old or older

set A group of something, such as exercises; often ten pushups is one set

technique The method or way to perform a judo move

Index

1 2 3 4 5 6 7 8 9 0 Printed in the U.S.A. 4 3 2 1 0 9 8 7 6 5